Golden Threads

Golden Threads

By Uranbileg Batjargal

atmosphere press

A word from the author

Severance. Threshold. Incorporation. In some native traditions, these are the three stages one must go through to come into one's full power. Sometimes they are called vision quests. Soul journeys. Rites of passages. The embarking on a new phase of life.

My severance phase reached its peak during a sacred ceremony in the mountains of Colorado, United States, at a vision quest program organized by School of Lost Borders, an organization that empowers individuals to claim their place within society and the natural world responsibly and respectfully. I arrived as an orphan child who had been separated at birth, as a Mongolian living in America, as a woman who lost her husband, with questions about where I belonged. I emerged from this profound experience with an understanding that I could belong everywhere if I shift the way I saw myself in the world. I sat in a circle with incredible guides and fellow seekers, shared our stories, wept together, and mirrored each other. I was asked to examine my beliefs, identities and attachments. Those experiences, among other powerful journeys, were the genesis for this collection.

What led me to attending my first vision quest was a sudden divorce; however, perhaps the severance started at my birth, when a hospital made a mistake and handed me over to a family of not my own blood. Although I was with the "other" family only for about three weeks, my body remembers and longs for them deeply. I've always struggled to belong with my own blood family. I eventually left my home country at the age of 19 to start a new life I could finally call my own and escape the desperation of a former Soviet Union state.

For the threshold phase of the vision quest, I fasted in solitude for four days on a mountain top. As I sat alone at my threshold, I felt both extremely terrified and immeasurably held by the surrounding natural beauty. I was gifted with songs. I started writing. I received a new name: Weaver of the Golden Thread. I did not fully understand the meaning of this name, but I felt I finally found a belonging, in a web of life where all beings are connected, fully accepted and loved. I thought I was ready for incorporation. But the threshold phase lasted longer than I thought it would. I fell in love with someone and poured all of my newborn self into this newfound love.

When the illusion ended, it felt as if everything returned to my beginning of severance. I was orphaned again. It would be two years before I could go on a second vision quest in the same mountains. There, I finally understood what it means to weave the golden thread. Integrating my soul into my body. Embracing my feminine and masculine parts. Remembering the lives I've lived and forgotten. Honoring the ancestors I've denied and run away from.

As I share this collection of poems and prose with you, my personal journey is in the incorporation phase. I am learning to love without expectations, to live without fear and to connect without having to fight, flee or freeze. I am learning to cry like an infant, to laugh and play like a child, to love and shine like a beautiful maiden, and to speak and act like an elder with wisdom and experience. It is a journey filled with magic, passion and hope amongst confusions, detours and disappointments. This journey is not only of my own, but also that of my lineage and my community. By being true to who we are and by expressing all aspects of us freely, lovingly, respectfully and kindly, we heal ourselves and heal each other.

I hope this collection will guide you through an inner landscape, where your soul may find a jewel, a rest, a nourishment or an inspiration. I am honored to be a companion for you on this path.

Table of Contents

I. Severance

Bridge of Questions

II. Threshold

Bridge of Revelations

III. Incorporation

Part I. Severance

Each moment is an opportunity to let go.

Free yourself from the cords.
Unloose
Yourself from the suffocations of limiting
Beliefs.

The ones you inherited.
The ones
Whispered while you were asleep.
Too naïve to know any better.

The ones that were gifts.

Sever each
Gently.
Shed
The old skin.

You are far more than what you
Fit yourself into.

Encounter with the Snake

Snake does not know it is killing you
It bites only to protect self.
I am who I am, says snake
While its venom burns vicious fire through your veins
Snake runs away fearing your dying heart.

Sometimes you look for snake
Tempt it
Sometimes it finds you
Suddenly
In your most blissful moment.

There are no answers to
Why you met
Why it bit
Why it hurts
There is only
Your struggle
To stay alive.

If the poison does not kill you
You've transformed yourself
The pain and the struggle were worth it
To find your place in the world
Once bitten and survived
You turn into medicine
Healing others who've been bitten.

Last Lovemaking

I wept.
Maybe because
It was the first time
In a long while
Maybe because
It was the last time
I knew.

Sweetness ends in bitter tears
Through it all you are dry
Silent withdrawal
Seedless parting.

Feelings I evoked in you
I will never know
No one will ever know
Even you don't know.

Feelings you invoked in me
The whole world will know.

Cats, Husbands, Fathers

I watched through the window. Cat's little head nestled against old man's shoulder. My husband looked on. Old man was my father.

I was certain of that though I also knew it was impossible. It was just like many other little things that I was certain of, though I also knew they were impossible.

Like the first time I saw my husband, I was certain that he would be my husband. But I also knew it was impossible. Our marriage did not last beyond the 7-year itch. At least his itch led him to a true love. They say that the third time is the charm. I was not too happy about being his second wife but very happy about being his second half. There was so much promise of love, new lands, and growing old togethers. But no one warned me that I would become the second guess, second thought, second best, second class, second ex-wife, to second hand on a dating market. The experience surely caused second degree burn to my heart but with second wind brought a second chance at a life that is my own.

When we adopted our first cat, I knew that her little head belonged nestled against my shoulders. My left side was her favorite. At the same time, I knew it was impossible. I was allergic to cats. Her affection brought me much joy and much suffering. Every morning I woke up with a stuffed nose and hives on my neck and face. But every morning I felt her body right on my heart, transmitting warmth that I had not experienced from another being, so directly, so freely. Even this suffering and blessing did not last long. Seven weeks after she entered my life, she left it suddenly. It was a mammary tumor, breast cancer for felines. Too advanced to cure. I cried. Felt sorry for all her nipples that never fed kittens but attracted this horrible disease instead.

Last time I saw my father, I was certain that it was the last time.
I didn't want to see him again anyways. Could not bear to look
at his despair and shame. Could not bear to smell the sourness
of his soul, drenched in cheap vodka; too comfortable in a thick
muck of self-hatred and anger toward the world. But I also knew
it was impossible to be the last time. His face haunts my dreams.
Occasionally he blesses me. Sometimes I catch his expression on
my own reflection in the mirror, which delights and terrifies me.
At least half of me is made of him. It is a matter of DNA. Perhaps
more than half of me is made of him. His love for words. A big
black mole we both have on our faces. His charm, intelligence,
brilliance. His amazing ability to speed walk over rocky fields
like a wild mountain goat. Beautiful large brown eyes. Rather
thin hair. Delicate but talented hands. All of these I carry in my
body.

In this life, now, I have no cats, no husbands, no fathers. But in
another life that I watch through the window, cat's little head is
nestled against old man's shoulder as my husband looks on. Old
man is my father. I am certain of this, though I also know it is
impossible.

Button

That day
You sewed button on my jeans
With so much focus
Tiny part of your tongue between your teeth
I thought
"Oh, how much this man loves me!"

I called it
The button of love.

Since then
You pressed gold button in my heart
With so much force
Raised voice shooting like a needle through
"There is a hole."
Broken promise twisting the thread
"There is a hold."
Calls in-between ignored
"There is a hope."

I called it
The button of pain.

Button on my jeans
Still hanging on
Shall I call it
Strength?

Button in my heart
Still hanging on
Shall I call it
Sorrow?

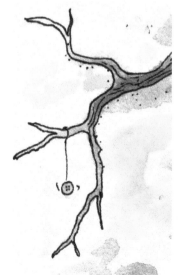

Cord

There still is a cord
  Connected to you
    Pulls when you hurt
      Pulses when you laugh

I feel its tug
  No matter how far away you are
    I hear its tune
      No matter how silent we've become.

They say I need to cut it
  To move on to a better future
    But every time I try
      A thicker one grows.

Connected to you
  I don't know
    Since when
      Till when

Maybe
  For this season
    A few more
      Maybe
        For this lifetime
          A thousand more.

What if, the key is to let it be?
  No cutting
    No feeding
      Just being.

How Far Can You Run?

How far away from your father can you run? His legs are longer. He took you to the green hill with old rocks where tasty berries grow. He taught you how to find a cone with nuts. He brought you a green dress with white trim and embroidered red roses from a trip to Moscow. With the bubble gum you tasted for the first time.

At family gatherings he asked me to sing. "You can do it yourself." Without a chorus. "Let your voice be heard." Sing as loud, as soft as you want. He taught me how to sing like me. I was often angry at having to sing. Like a little doll who entertains strangers—supposedly my family. I sang because I loved him. His handsome face would light up, his delicate hands holding a big jar of beer. White trinkets of foam around his red lips. His dazzling eyes glow mellow, carried away by my lullaby.

I mostly sang about fathers. "My father the horseman." "My father the singer." "May my father live forever." Mom hated it. She resented that my voice never carried the same melody when I sang about mothers. There would be a high pitch and a mechanical sound. "Don't let me find you," the mother in me says. She never loved you. Remember the things she said. I was better off with the family that mistakenly took me from the hospital soon after my birth. I brought nothing but trouble and mischief. I should be grateful that she kept me.

Poison. Her words were. They made my singing voice dry up. They brought up odd notes not in harmony with my heart. I wanted to run away so fast that no sound could catch up. I wanted to hide so deep that no light could find me. But how can you hide away from either your mother or father? They are where you come from, aren't they?

Don't Leave Just Yet

I want to touch your body
Stroke your soft skin
Through a dark forest of
Your rising hair
To greet you
Home.

Come inside
Visit this cave of mystery
You are meant to be
Here.
All of you
Welcome.

Take me
To the other world
Beyond yours and mine
Take me
To where we come from.

Don't leave just yet
Stay
I can hold you
When you are
Soft.

My restless feet long to dance
My invisible wings shimmer in furry white

Oh, mysterious bird!
Meat eating
Fire spitting
Where inside me
Do you sleep?

Banana Episode

White flesh of a banana
Flirting in a yellow dress
Sandy feeling in my mouth
Tingly pressure in my chest.

Last night, like all other nights
My body nestled against yours
A warm core solid like a maple.

Burden woke me early this morning
From a sweet dream where I lived
Free and beyond
There, banana grows from maple tree, wears blue kimono.

Here on chestnut table
Underdressed banana
A ThinkPad holds
My shaky fingers to keyboard.
In this world,
This is what makes sense
This is what is asked for
This is what is valued.

You enter
Half-naked, no pants
Your own banana
Loose between your legs
Not a maple, nor a chestnut
Sharp eyes land on table.

"Take your banana off my table!" you say.

Your screech
A weapon too sharp for a morning like this.
Your words
Explode
My fruit
My bosom
The beast within.

I sweep the banana off table
To the floor
A mere veneer, pretentious imitation of wood
Glossy grey surface you and I walk upon.

"How dare you?" you scream.
Ninja daggers of ancient Chinese clan
Aimed at my core
The hungry one inside.

Heat steams from your heavy presence
Piercing laser in your eyes
That once used to gaze at me
With soft glow.

"Pick it up!" you cry.

I walk to the banana
I smash it with my foot
Smear it over the floor.

The sad grey floor needed some
Color
Shine
Aliveness
Borrowed from a banana.

Your heavy shadow pounces on mine
Your hands don't dare to touch me but strangle my silhouette.

"How dare you?
You don't know what I am capable of!"

I know exactly what you are capable of.
I am not afraid.
"Show me.
Show me who you really are!"

Arms against your chest
The beast is unleashed
You lose balance.

I have this strength.

Once in an elevator
I pushed a man who tried to kiss me
With a force that cracked a steel door open.

Once in a dream
I pushed my father off a balcony
Watched his drunken brain splatter
On a pavement five floors below.

Once in a park
I pushed my then spouse
At discovery of his false heart
He fell on the grass
Marked green streaks on his khaki pants.

I have this strength.

I am not afraid of the love, passion, inspiration

You brought
Willingly or grudgingly
True and false.

I am not afraid of the violence, suppression, oppression
You showed
Passively or aggressively
Now and then.

I am not afraid of
Your supposed strength over my small frame
I am not afraid of
Your departure and the loneliness to follow.

I am afraid of
Losing my color
Dimming my light
Becoming lifeless
Like a soft sweet banana.

A Kiss Remembered

Mother, you came to my dreams last night. You were somehow kinder and softer. Your lips were not as thin. They smiled instead of their usual tight grimace. You kissed my forehead. Strange yet familiar. I remember a kiss just like this when I was a young girl. After we came back from the emergency room. The one you took me to by bus, from the village we spent summers at. I don't remember the bus ride, the hospital hall, the doctor, the needle, or the stitches. I remember the moment a stocky neighbor boy waved his arm at me and something flew toward me. Warm liquid ran down my cheek. When I touched my face and held my hand before me, I saw red. I ran home to you. Innocence was still alive then.

You slapped me. Hands that were supposed to hold and caress me. Your hands told me I was bad. Sharp-tongued. Spiteful. Troublemaker. Provoker. Peace disturber. I was the sling that shot a sharp rock to my forehead. Above my right eyebrow. I had asked for it. By being so naughty. By playing with boys. By calling them names. By drawing out anger so natural to them. I caused you to land your strong hand on my cheek. Now I made you feel like a bad mother. At least the rock missed my eyes. How would you handle a burden of a blind child?

I don't remember the motherly duties you masterfully performed to ensure my survival. Getting to the hospital, completing the paperwork, bringing me back, putting me to bed. Perhaps you even carried me. I don't remember. I do remember the kiss you bestowed on my forehead as I fell asleep. "Oh," I thought. "She still loves me." Even though I am so bad.

Words Unsaid

The other day
You whispered
"So beautiful"
While kissing my breasts.

Did you mean them
Or me
Or are they the same?

The day before
You wrote
"Will you forgive me?"

Did you mean
For you being late on a date
Or for being late in my life?

Years have gone by
Since our paths first crossed
Since the day my kiss took you by surprise
Since the day you rescued me from snow and shirts came off.

Who am I to you?
Behind the doors that don't open
Between the days we don't meet
Beyond the words you don't say.

The House You Didn't Build for Us

The house you didn't build for us
Sits on a tiny hill
Watching a shore of a foamy sea
There is a willow
Weeping in the back yard
A red maple is burning bright too.

Sun sets on front door
You on the front porch
A mug of scotch
Me with a martini
Dirty and salty.

In your eyes
I see the setting sun
Two birds flying toward the horizon
Where today ends and tomorrow comes
I hear their cries
Calling for each other.

In your lips
I taste the blood that boils in your head
All the passion you could not say
By words, by songs.

Your tight shoulders and heavy neck
Burdened with what you refuse to unload
But can't claim as your own
Unspoken loyalty to your father
Whose limbs once stopped moving.

Occasionally
Your grip was strong

Your touch gentle and kind
But often
Your words were harsh
Your steps too gingerly.

Your hands that never lifted bricks
For the house you didn't build for us
Held perfect contradictions of hope and despair
An ancient mudra undiscovered, never taught.

The house you never built for us
Stands tall in another world
I go there often in my dreams
To bless the trees that never grew
Smell the roses that never bloomed
Kiss the foreheads of children we never had.

They say that to build a house
You must lay one brick at a time.

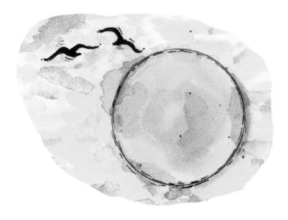

Search and A House Shoe

I often have a nightmare about getting lost. I search in vain in foggy places, abandoned buildings, dark hallways of giant mansions. I look for my room in a place that looks like shared housing or a dormitory. I look for my belongings when I eventually find my room.

First memory I have of being lost in waking life is the day you spanked me with a house shoe. It had wooden soles. I was in kindergarten, only 15 minutes away from our house. I sat with the building guard after all the kids and teachers left for the day. He made a compote from raisins and poured me a cup from a grey metal teapot. It was less sweet than usual. The guard was an old man with hunched back, wrinkly skin and long grey hair. He was kind. It had become our evening routine to sit together in an empty kindergarten building, sharing a pale compote. Another evening you and father forgot to pick me up.

"Today, I am not going to wait," I said to myself. "Today I will find my home, on my own." I then left the guard and the building behind. Walked through the neighborhood that seemed so familiar and small before this solitary walk. I was lost. I wandered hopeful. "This next building will be the home," I would cheer myself. When it wasn't, I would wander further hoping that the next building was the one. Dozen more buildings. Farther from my home, I started panicking. Then hysterically cried. I don't remember how I was found. There were policemen involved. I recall the wrinkly kind face of the kindergarten guard, now relieved from its worries. I recall then the cold hard wooden sole of the house shoe, against my naked bottom, my body stretched across your lap, face touching the floor. "I promise I won't run away again," I cried.

I didn't keep that promise. In my imagination, I ran away a thousand times, successfully. In reality, I ran away only a few times. Once to my Aunt Saruul's house. She comforted me and assured me that I could stay with them as long as I wanted to. Then she called you to come and collect me. Once to my best friend's house. Her parents called you too. The final run was across the country borders, in a winged machine. No one at my destination was going to call you to hand me over. It was a home I found for myself, far away from the wooden sole.

I often have a nightmare about getting lost. Looking for my home, wandering though empty unfamiliar buildings. I still take the lonely run to liberty, even if the end of the dream is to find myself stark naked. I always wake up before the wood touches my flesh.

Games We Played

Hanky panky
Hide and seek
Catch me if you can
Your favorite games are not the ones I want to play.

Not with you
Not with anyone
Not anymore.

A friend
You called me often
And you didn't add
Benefits.
The words rolled off your tongue
Like the shirt and pants slid off your body.

A lover
I called you occasionally
While meaning
Beloved.
The word choked in my throat every time
Expectations are roadblocks on the way to love.

We didn't get to play house
Instead lots of jump rope.

Simon said:
Bend over
On all fours
Turn around
Contort yourself spineless.

I straddled the square of your body
Thinking I would hopscotch through

To reach a safe place called home
I threw the unlucky piggy
A beanbag of fortune
All the wrong directions.

You were the rock
I was the scissors
Without the paper
One is always an unwelcome alien
Stranded behind an impenetrable wall.

There was no chair in your heart
For me to claim
No matter how much
I pranced and danced
To the music only I could hear.

No need to tag anyone
With names they don't want to take on
I lost my balance
While hopping through
The court of no courting.

Too many games were played at once
No rules were there to keep things fair.

Now, not many memories to get over
No photos to rip or delete from phones
Just a sore heart
A bystander victim
Today's loser
Tomorrow's winner.

Both of us are tired.
Game over.

Marriage to Shame

My father was married to Shame. It first arrived in an innocent looking bottle, gifted by someone who admired him. The bottle was almost as beautiful as he. Bubbly, vibrant, fragrant and strong. But the Shame was bigger than Genie. It did not listen to its master. Once unleashed from the bottle, it shadowed over the rest of my family, changing us into unrecognizable characters.

First, it latched on to my mother. In her vagina, specifically. She could no longer be satisfied with what his virility had to offer. Then the Shame moved into her mouth. She could not stop vomiting vicious fires of blame, belittlement, and bitterness.

Then the Shame took over my older brother. It made his fists tighten, teeth clench, and legs kick high like a Kung Fu master. He made loud sounds in the kitchen, slapped doors, broke windows.

It was scary when the Shame moved into me. It mostly visited me in dreams. Gave me powers to lift a giant rock, smash my father's skull and splatter his brain on a concrete. Push him out of a balcony on the 5th floor of the Soviet style apartment we lived in. Stab his heart with a giant kitchen knife. Drown him in a tub not big enough to bathe my little brother.

It was scariest when the Shame moved into my darling little brother. It covered his innocent beautiful eyes with thick clouds of sadness. Made his thin body tremble with fear and confusion. Instilled in him a belief that something was horribly wrong, particularly with him. That the horror was here to stay.

Marriage to Shame is a mistake. Divorce is a prescription unless you want death. Leave. Run for your life. A new, single, celibate, safe life. A life that is your own.

Insatiable Hunger, Cause Unknown

I am still hungry
   Don't feed me instant noodles and other morsels
   Salad alone can't satisfy my body
   Still water won't quench my thirst.

I want a feast, a celebration, an indulgence.

Sacrificial lamb, tender and sweet
   Young life saved without mercy from dry meat and feeble bones
   Gold potatoes, rich and fresh
   Harvest of blistered hands through seasons of drought
   Fine wine, luscious and smooth
   Fruit of patient waiting in dark lonely cellar, aged to bitter sweetness.

I don't want your teasing
   Glimpse of white flesh through a lacy dress
   I want your breasts exposed, no fabric to hide, no wires to prison
   I want to suck them perky to offer pure milk of life.

Don't tempt me with your
   Sweet lips, buttery tongue, and silky hands alone
   I want you inside me, with your explosive forces
   Hairy, sticky, hardened penetration.

Take me with all of you, in your rough tough, rushed slow,
   tender forceful ways
   Feel all of me, in my chafed cracked, creamy weepy, bloody
   sloshy waves.

No holding back
No hesitance
If you want to love me

Love me all the way.

On Bread, Milk, Meat, and Potatoes

I am all grown up now. But I can't eat bread or drink milk. My body does not tolerate gluten or lactose. Sometimes I wonder how I managed as a child. During that time when all we had to eat was two loaves of bread and a liter of milk per week; those were the portions determined to be adequate quantity for a family of five. It was my job to get up at 6 a.m. and wait in the line, holding the meal tickets. I am not an early riser, and I hated this chore. While in line, I longed for the good old days of communism, where the fridge was always full. Mandarins, apples, eggs on Sundays. I didn't understand why they said the old regime was bad. New regime meant hungry belly and I'd much rather have a full fridge. I daydreamed about the day when abundance would arrive. While skipping in place to keep myself warm.

One winter we had a lot of potatoes. Too excited, I boiled a big batch. I must have eaten at least ten. Certainly, enough to make me sick. I could not even look at a potato for five years. One fall a sheep stayed on our balcony. Father had brought the sheep back from his visit to the countryside. He explained the mutton, once cured and dried, should be enough to get us through the winter. But the sheep kept crying and when the silence came at the mercy of the sharp knife's edge in uncle's hand, I felt a relief. The peace did not last long, as I was told to clean the intestines. Pass a piece of raw liver through the freshly severed intestines until all waste is removed. The clean intestines were filled with the sheep's blood and flesh and made into a sausage. I could not eat the sausage, even though it smelled delicious and I was hungry.

More food supplies started appearing. Farmers' market bloomed in a square nearby. They sold vegetables and meat from the back of big trucks. One day, I went to buy a cabbage.

When my turn in the line came, I raised both of my arms, one holding money, the other reaching out for the bag with the cabbage. I was wearing a skirt. I felt a hand reach from under the truck, touching my body in places I later found to be sacred. My instinct was to kick the owner of the hand. I tried my best, but it didn't affect the caresser. I screamed for help but people behind me stared, annoyed at the scene and the noise. They, too, wanted a cabbage. Or maybe meat. It couldn't wait. Mom made a stir-fried dish from the cabbage, but I couldn't eat it, even though it smelled delicious and I was hungry.

Years after the adventures of potatoes, sausages, and cabbages, I made my own household and learned to cook decent food. My husband always praised my cooking. Apparently, I was a natural. At mixing spices without measuring and cooking meals without timing. But food remained synonymous with survival. I cooked a dinner for two, in a modern kitchen with appliances I can't name, using abundant meat and vegetables enough to feed a family of five. I dreamt about the day when nourishment would arrive.

Conversation with The Shadow

Shadow,
    Sometimes you are larger than me
      Sometimes smaller

Shadow,
    You appear only when there is some light
      Someone's love
        A kind word
          Promise of a better tomorrow
            Trust in my inner voice
              Then you show up.

Shadow,
    I don't see you in the dark, embraced by the thick black fog
      where I come from
      Shadow,
        I don't feel you when I sit naked in my lonely
        cell, covered in dirt
          Shadow,
            I don't hear you when I cry in despair
            of my perpetual chagrin.

Are you really part of me?
    Or are you a thing between me and someone else?
      Are you a gift or a curse?
        Or simply my relation to the world outside?

Inside me
    You and I are one
      Outside me
        You talk dirty
          You slam doors and burn bridges
            Inside me
               You and I don't exist

Outside me
    You are farther than I want to
    hold.

They say to be happy I must face you
    To wrestle with you and defeat you
      Strangle your neck, tumble your legs
        Pull your hair and knock out your teeth.

I stand still
    Feeling your weight
      Heavy and delicious
      I wait for a sign
        A flag of any color.

Wishful Vengeance

At times I wanted to kill you
Sever your bull head from your thick neck
Feel your blood run down my fingers
See your eyes beg for mercy.

But then I wanted to hold you close
Kiss every millimeter of your dark skin
Your crooked teeth
Your pouty lips
The cancer scar on your neck.

I wish I could've simply loved you
Showered you with pure affection
But my love fumed

To get even
Break your heart
Tear your skin open
So that you
Feel my pain.

Wasted Land

Barren grey field
No sign of life
Not a blade of grass
Survived

Fire of regret
Vengeance
Emptied the field
Destroyed the birches.

Once
A field full of
Purple and yellow wildflowers
Emerald grass
Lightning bugs

Now
Everything is
Burned to ashes.

Only a sliver
Of a new moon above.

Bridge of Questions

Where Do the Lost Socks Go?

To a dusty corner behind a giant machine, crushed against the
wall?
In a spiraling pipe that sucks away the dirt, detergent, and
water that carries them?
Into a space between the drier and the washer
floating in alternate dimension
stolen by one who wanted to store
holiday gifts for one who is loved?

Did they get tired of
being stepped into, trampled upon
shoved into tight shoes they don't want to walk in?
Did they want a new partner
who doesn't look and feel so much like themselves?
Did they need a new life
without so much sweat and stink?

Did they find enlightenment
ascend to the other world
for being humbled to the ground
having sufficiently touched the feet chakra?

Where do the lost socks go?
Why don't they take the journey in pairs?
Where should all the
half-lost, left-behind, sad looking, grieving socks go?

Even if they are
perfectly clean, barely worn, and genuinely warm
Are they no good on their own?

When the Wind Blows

Sakura,
You fall on my face ever so gently
Can dying be so graceful?

Sakura,
Your branches are splendid when half naked
Am I beautiful, even robbed of joy?

White, pink, green
Your delicate flowers
Dark, pale, grey
My disillusioned spirit.

Powerful wind blew away your petals
Passing love broke all my hopes.

I ache with emptiness at your nakedness
You weep white petals of compassion for my pain
Next year I will come when you are in full bloom
Know that my heart will be full of joy again.

When You Need Sweetness

Flight attendant offered me ice cream for dessert. Plastic chicken and salty orzo had left me thirsty. I received the gift with a smile and swallowed without inhaling. My body does not welcome lactose. But today I needed sweetness. Uniformed shepherds had herded me through gates and patted me down. Random selection, they said. Have I always been the one chosen? I am on my way to a new land, to answer a calling of my heart. I can't fly on my own yet, so I got on an airplane. What will I find when I get there?

The man next to me also took ice cream. He panicked when he could not find a spoon. I showed him the secret place under the lid where a tiny paper spoon laid. The man grinned with delight. His fingers escaped a messy dip to the milky mud. His body, too, could not welcome lactose. I caught the small grimace just before the ice cream crossed the borders of his lips.

We all need sweetness.
Especially when carried away
Helplessly
In an unreliable vessel
To an unknown destination.

Part II. Threshold

Sit quietly.
Held by nature.
No voice to distract you.
No morsel to give you a false sense of nourishment.
No four walls, no illusions.
No safety.

Here,
You remember yourself.
Here,
You discover your truth.
Here,
You are utterly and completely loved.

Here,
You Die.
Here,
You Rebirth.

War and Beauty

Beauty awaits.
Behind the walls I built of fear that
Part of me plans to hurt me.

It awaits
Patiently, lovingly
It awaits
No expectations, only trust.

It waits for me
To disappear
To matter less
To muster courage
Emerge.

Break down the walls
Let the light flow
Embrace this part and that

Only when the war is over
I can be the beauty that I am.

Seeking

Too many times
I left the ground
Close to the moon
Comings and goings
Takeoffs and landings.

Nomad in me seeks
New places to visit, not to settle in
To hug the trees, not to timber them
To have a roof without doors
To start a fire that doesn't burn down forests.

Seeker in me searches
For a destiny
A place where
I will finally feel at home
In strange new lands
Welcoming and terrifying.

In everyone
I search for my Beloved
In beckoning grey eyes that promise tethering
In mesmerizing greens that hold the riches
In awakening blues that calls to possibilities
In grounding hazels that emit warmth of a sun
In centering blacks that invite to a mystery.

Where is the shine my soul will recognize?
Golden thread connected to my heart?

Then again
I get tired of the search
Comings and goings
Wear out this small frame.

This center is hardened from past blows
But awake to renewal
These windows are tired from passing winds
But hopeful for a fresh direction
These gateways are small; flashflood washed away its
inheritance
But open palms wait for new gifts
These pillars are born short and invisible
But ready for steady steps toward openness.

This is grace
To hold the opposites
To stand still at the threshold of
Arrival and departure.

As Above, As Below

Sometimes, I descend into a well in my back yard
Where lives a child
Deep underground
No sun can reach
Stone walls mildewed by perpetual rain
Empty cage
No fresh water, no visitors.

She cries for light
Shivers for a sun
Orphaned by the world
Afraid of her needs.

Grief is her best friend
Fear is the second best
Will someone come to bring new friends?
Joy and laughter, perhaps.

I invite her to come above
Offer her wings, songs, beauty
Sweetness.
She prefers to stay in the damp bottom of the well
Familiarity is a harsh comfort.

I long for her homecoming
But I won't pull her arms.
I visit, sit, breathe the moldy air
Hug her thin cold presence
Close to me.

I trust
She will take small steps toward me
Above the dark well
There is a sunny field.

Sour Well and Fresh Spring

I struggle with you for hours at night
Dead tree pressing against my chest
Oh, total stranger, I know you so well.

You arise in the dark
When my body is weak, my mind asleep
My spirit faraway in a magical land collecting mana.

You sit on my core
Turn my bed into a merry-go-around
Tell me never to rise again.

Life force bottled in my belly
Soured from churning
Is this an arak of horse milk to welcome a guest
Or to twist unsuspecting stomach?

This well is not fresh
No one drank from it for a while
This well is tired of its own reflection
Welcomes anything that looks, even the lost souls hungry for
sourness.

I ask the alien to leave me alone.
My half-awake mind escaped to a room where Jane sleeps.

I reach for the light. Lamps don't work.
I reach for the window. Hundred unfamiliar spirits play outside
with fireworks.
Innocent children departed too young?
Feeble elders, left too lonely?

What if, what if?

You are a part of me?
One I can allow in only when half-asleep
One with power to move beds, crush dreams, turn all lights off.

What if, what if?
The only way to have you go is to ask you to stay?
Let your weight crush the gates, fall to the bottom
Find a place where a fresh spring hides
Crack all blocks with the same desperation

So I can finally rise
Fresh and strong
Flowing and glowing.

In Good Company

Lean into what you want to run from
Reach out a hand, see if it really bites
Fall out of love with your struggle
Attachment no more to your own brokenness.

You've been loyal to your pain too long
All your companies are bored
Sad queen bound in an ice castle wants touch of sun on her
naked skin
Grieving maiden caged in loneliness needs embrace of dancing
grasses
Soldier in rusted armor weary from long fights yearns for
freedom of a pilgrim.

Wave them goodbye
Kiss them, hug them
Give them parting gifts if that's what you want
Saddle up their horses
Fill their bags with nourishment
To find a new home far from your own.

New guests want to enter your life
Through rib-framed doors, lash-curtained windows, light-filled
peepholes
Wherever else you will let them in
Joyful ones you don't believe you deserve
Dashing knight in red and green robe
Beautiful goddess in shimmering gold dress
Glamourous infant with soft belly and silver laughter.

They don't mind your dusty rug
Creaky floor, leaky roof, unpolished silver, rusted pots
Chipped cups, mismatched plates, forks without knives.

They don't mind any of it, darling
They only want your open arms and softened heart.

Drop your shoulders
Loosen your belly
Welcome them
Be in good company.

Old Self Must Die

The old self must die
To make place for the new

The fighting self must lower its swords
The hungry-for-love self must find nourishment within
The hardworking self can take a vacation
The always-want-to-be-right self can surrender to not knowing

The pleasing self must take on a new role
The pleading self must learn to speak the truth
The men-don't-want-me self must want herself first.

I have a voice.

I say
"Yes"
To my heart's longing
"More"
To my body's desire.

Sit in A Circle

Life invites you to a circle
To open your heart
To truly listen, at last
The divine flows
Through who speaks
Mirrors the parts
Neglected by your Self.

Let your eyes free
Vision beyond the ordinary
The one
Before you
Next to you
Farthest away from You.

Open your ears
To wisdom
Beyond the common
Weeping of this
Whisper of that
Thumping of the one Within.

Who brought you here?
Stars aligned
Wind blew to the North
Sun warmed the path.

Tears of sky
Down your cheek
Cool you awake.

Come
Sit in a circle with me
You are exactly where
You are meant to be.

Holding the Opposites

I walk this land with reverence

New leaves on a half-dead tree
Sky sheds tears of joy and grief
Sun shines through the clouds
Birds sing, then silent

Holding the opposites
Dark and light
Let them dance together
Holding the opposites
Sacred and profane.

A Place

Rock is rock
Water is water
One can't be the other.

Rock blocks water from flow
Water licks rock until it smooths.

This is life
Each has its place.

War starts when
Rock acts like water
Water tries to become rock.

Hear Me Out

Do not discount me because of my thin hair
Do not label me sick because I bear no fruit
Do not discard me based on my single weak limb
I am no different than You.

Each strand of my thin hair is just as precious as
Your thick, luscious, curly mess
Each leaf of my body births as much oxygen as
Your thorny, bushy heaviness.

I love my
Nakedness
Solitude
Fragility.

It is what makes me
Real
Vulnerable
Lovable.

I belong to this world as much as you do
I am a beloved to the divine as much as you are.

See my beauty.
If you can't
Question your vision
Not my substance.

Feel my preciousness.
If you can't
Examine your senses
Not my worth.

I live under this
Blue sky
Hot sun
Next to you.

I love under this
White moon
Dark night
With you.

On Breaking Free

Colorful clothes on a rope bathe in a warm sun
Say hello to their neighbors, whom they can't reach
For each is fastened by a clip
Thin torsos wave in the air
Wind is their only playful ally.

Harsh wind jolts me back to dusty Ulaanbaatar
Callused hands of my mother
Vacant eyes of my father
Browned ropes waiting for my only pair of pants
I was thirteen.

My hands in tepid water, kneading fabric
Dirt on my pants from rolling in mud
Rubbed against the hard washboard
Stains on sanitary cloth from my adulthood markings
Scrubbed even harder.

"I want to break free!" Purple Shorts say.
"I want to be worn with you" Yellow T-shirt giggles.
Next to each other they hang, unable to embrace
Their destiny left in the hands of the lady
Who hung them to dry, to be worn, to be useful.

I wanted to break free too
From
The washing, scrubbing, hanging
The dusts that won't let clothes to keep pure
From
The hungry stomach grateful for half frozen potatoes
The stench of mutton, slaughtered on a balcony; a winter's
bounty
From
The roaches who owned the house at night

The sighs and whines of the mother of three.

I wanted to be worn by a beautiful boy; wrap myself around his
bottom like a tightly fitting purple love
I wanted to be matched with a yellow T-shirt, whose dream
was to be worn with me
I wanted an ally as free as the wind, as warm as the sun
I wanted an arm to unclip me from the line, to be useful.

I sit on a porch of my little hut
Whisper my wishes to the colorful clothes:
"You will be free, don't you worry."

When all that binds you breaks with the wild wind
You will shred to thin fiber
When all your colors fade
You will become all colors.

You will break free
To belong to the thread of life itself.

Goodbye

So, this is the sunset.
That started before our "Hello."
Two strangers we met.
Two teachers we part.

Banana Waves

I lie on the floor unable to move
Banana tree dances with the wind
She calls me and waves
"Come out to play"
I am bound to my old belongings.

"The world is a scary place," I was told
Every creature is out to get you, to suck the life out of you
To dim your light and eat you alive
If you dare to love.

Mosquito bites; kill it!
Roaches crawl; crush them!
Pretty flowers; pluck them!
Wild potatoes; dig them out, fry them!

I was taught to fight
To survive in this world
I learned to run
Grab everything edible on the way out.

"Come out to play," banana leaf says
"Trust this world you are part of
No creature is here to hurt you
Rain will wash away your crusted armors
Birds will teach you a new song of awakening
Fish will offer her life to ease your hunger
Fruit of my being will gift you a smooth dessert."

Banana leaf waves and waves
My doubting chest waits and waits
Is the world really a safe place?
Is it really okay to be me?

Rise to Faith

You've been
Patient, silent, bowing
For too long
The spirit of the mighty in you
Can stay dormant
No longer.

Wake up!
Be bold, dance, roar
Raise dust under your feet
Remain awake and strong
When daemons come to wrestle.

Dream big
Take that step towards your edge
Jump off that cliff
See how your wings grow
Take you to a new height.

Even if you fall
There is love waiting underneath
Ocean to catch you, hold you
Lull you into peace.

Don't be afraid of
What the worst could look like
Instead imagine
What the best will feel like.

Call from An Angel

Woke up again at 3am
No later
No sooner
Moonless sky
No star.

All light hides behind the dark veil
I conjured around my eyes.

Loneliness rises again
Fear lurks an inch behind
Pressure of my tired old story is
Stronger than migraines I've had since thirteen
The stench of self-inflicted wound is
Sharper than anchovies on last night's pizza.

Sweet dark wine
Numb me, soothe me
Flow purity of Jesus through my veins
I can stand the thickness of it all
So long as I am entangled inside the whole.

Mother, you called me a petulant child; denied my
independence
Threw me outside the circle; beat me up with a wooden shoe
Because I wanted to find a home.

Slapped my face; laughed at my dripping blood
Your words cut deeper than the sharp rock above my right
brow.

In this slimy tar of a moment
I struggle, strangle, sink, freeze. All at once.
I hear an angel's call; answer to my prayer?

"I love you sister, beautiful, courageous Soul."

I forget my intoxication
I transcend chains of my lineage, curses of my mother.

I am not defined by half-remembered stories of my childhood
Name they called, shame I carried.

I am what I see through the eyes of my sisters.
I am the angel who called me last night.

Partners

I want to be your rain partner
Naked or clothed
Run through the washing water
Recognize, allow, investigate, nurture.

Tear drops on my skin
Your sacred suffering is mine too
Promises made, broken, kept
Dreams shattered, dreamt again
Long before this life.

I want to be your bonding partner
On top or underneath
To feel you
Essence to essence
Without a weight
Without a pressure
To hold gently
The preciousness of togetherness.

I want to be your tantric partner
Eyes open or closed
Gaze into your hazel sparkles
Travel beyond the eternity
Vanish into oneness
To unite with you in body
On top of a mountain
Next to a river
Inside a cave
In ecstasy
Fill the land with love
Feed all creatures.

I want to be your questing partner

In a desert or a valley
Send you a hello in the mornings
A colorful stone in a shape of a heart
Receive a hello in the evenings
A stick, a cone, a treasure you find
To sing over the mountains
Hear the land echo
Multiply every vibration in a hundred
To greet you at a threshold of new beginnings

To witness your journey to the north, east, south, west
Aging, dying, birthing, stepping into your purpose
To mirror your gifts, dances, songs
To see you as the divine sees you.

All of these
I want to be
For you
With you.

Message to Self

I must not
Rush like flash flood
Destroy canyon

I must
Stand like ancient tree
Wait as new seed
Lands.

I must not
Burst like hot volcano
Melt ground

I must
Hold like good earth
Nourish trees that
Grow.

I must not
Blast like great storm
Create chaos

I must
Flow like gentle river
Water roots that
Bloom.

Weaving A New Story

In my hand
Dry pokey bush
Dirty roots dangling like a beet just dug
Half my height
Arms reach to seven directions
Slender numerous fingers.

In my pocket
Yarns of four colors
Garnet, turquoise, sapphire, chrysoprase
Carry strength of four legged
Sheep, goat, alpaca, yak.

Yarns flow into branches
Come together through my fingers
Envelop the root, the arm, the fingers
Weave a story of
Not belonging, getting lost
Being too little, too much
Not having love, direction, acceptance.

This old story must go into the sacred fire tonight
To be offered to spirits
To be honored in silence
To make place for the new.

Finding My Wings

Walk in woods behind green pond
Frogs sing with birds
I cry with sky.

Behind my shoulder there is an ancient pain
Fantom of wings I once had and lost
Arrows of jealousy shot through my heart
Its poison spread
I forgot who I was.

At my foot
White bone glitter with rain drops
Fraction of a spine, bare flesh
Few steps away
Dragon foot, four toes, scaly skin
Full flesh, fatty gloss, repulsive stench.

I mistake you for scattered bones of fried chicken
Left from weekend party of youth
I dismiss you as fragment of my imagination
Borrowed from the Games of Thrones.

But,
You are here.
You are real.

Bone of my bones
Flesh of my flesh
Blood of my blood
Skin of my skin.

I find you
Piece by piece

Femur, scapula, beak
Spine, sternum, more feet.

Feathers, iridescent black
Feathers, black and blue
My hands making a trail to mystery.

Feathers, bored stuck in mud
Feathers, waiting for new feather's arrival
My hands reaching layers, invisible to naïve eyes.

Feathers, kissing
Feathers, crossing mighty knights' swords
My hands holding the love and the fight alike.

Feathers, sweeping good witch's broom
Feathers, floating slimy pond, seducing frogs
My hands embracing the enchantress and the goddess.

Yes,
I fell from grace once
Yes,
I was killed more than once
My heart broke countless times

But
I find my broken bones and feathers
Weave my wings
Claim a new flight.

House I Built

I built myself
A home in a desert
With green tarp, white ropes
Leaning against sharp boulders
I felt
Safe.

Great wind came
Blew it away
Cut the ropes
Tore the tarp.

I cussed the wind
Threw rocks at the tarp
Flung the ropes at my shadow
Curled into a ball on the ground
I felt
Homeless.

I surrendered.

Wind is my teacher
Sky is my roof
Earth is my floor
This body is my home.

I am
Free.

Song of My Heart

I came to this mountain to find a simple truth
Spent four days four nights
In the company of my aloneness.

I lived without walls
Witnessed by sky, blown by wind
Blazed by sun, held by rocks
I found
Where home is.

When my body shed
All the false notes it carried
I first dreamt
Of all the perilous injections
Strange melodies
Sizzling pizza, dripping ice cream
Sparkling wine, popping soda
I learned
What nourishment is.

When I saw only my shadow
Mirroring every move I make
In light and in darkness
I knew
Whose face to hold in my palms
Whose lips to tenderly kiss
Whose heart I want beating next to mine.

When my legs shook, hands bled
Head spun, stomach growled
I felt
What body is
I held

Each part intimately
Numb, alive
Strong, fragile
Precious
Hungry for caress.

When I heard only crying birds, buzzing flies
Whispering breeze, silent mountains
I finally tuned in
To the song that flows through the veins of my heart

The song that's been waiting for me to wake up
To claim my place
To crowd out the doubt.

I start singing
As if it is my last day
Alive.

Waking Up to A Golden Thread

Lids shut
Lingering to last night's dream
Threads pull
Dancing in golden shimmer

Get up, get up!
Grandmother worked all night
Grandfather lights her creation

From branch to branch new bridge is built
Among green leaves golden flowers blossom
Mysterious embroidery on stump of a dead tree
Call out to the symbols hidden in your chest

Eyes open
Weaver born.

My Life Has A Purpose

Vigil began at sunset. I sat in a circle of stones and pinecones and prayed for a Vision. I danced with the moon. Listened to the silence of the other world. Trees revealed the ancient shapes of shamans, animals, guardians. Grass danced to an enchanting tune. I became one with them. They named me: Weaver of The Golden Thread.

Trees came alive. They whispered:

Your life has a purpose
To weave a golden thread
To your, his, her, their hearts.

Fly with the Hawk
Sit with the Owl
Sing with the Hummingbird.

Weave the golden thread
Lead them to their home.

Prayer Upon Waking

May the moon light my way as I walk this path
May the land anchor me to my core when I despair
May my shadow dance with me when I feel lonely
May the sun rise again to renew my trust in continuity

May the sky birth me to freedom, a destination for all
May the fire ignite my remembrance
May the birds teach me a new way of being
May my family hold my spirits high as we feast together

May I weave golden threads without tangling
May I walk gently.

A seeker
I remain
A love
I return.

Weave the Golden Thread

I woke up this morning feeling cold and alone. Couldn't feel my toes. Owl hoots nearby. I lie on grass, damp from morning dew. Sun warms my face and gives me a hope. I turn my head to the left. Stare at the triangular blue tarp. Sun shines on it too.

Golden threads on the branches of a pine tree under which I am housed. Golden threads on the dead branches where a red bandana from REI and yellow underwear from Hanky Panky lay. Hummingbird flutters by. My every morning's wake up call for the last four days. Then my friend squirrel comes. Sings his chirpy songs. Black birds of various sizes fly above. One of them is Hawk.

Everything is calling me by my name. Waving "hello" to my homecoming.

Birds above sing, "Weave the golden thread." The squirrel chimes in, "Lead them to their hearts." I respond to their calling in a silent prayer. I vow to myself to live up to my new name.

Bridge of Revelations

You Are the Middle

Lean into the first woman
Mother of my mother's mother
Rest in her bosom
Before taint of betrayal darkened the canvas.

Orphan, born to orphans
Believed from conception a story of not belonging
Permeable soft tissues of my essence
Carried forward violence of
Imagined bloodshed.

The same blood that gave me life
Injected doses of poisons
My body could
Neither develop immunity nor die from it.
The river of my being
Dams, rocks, occasional rainbows
Visit of a hummingbird.

The first woman carries the purity of feminine essence
Asks me to wake up
To my own power
Milk from her breasts purify
Clogs of this polluted river.

Face your mother, in her orphaned beliefs
She is not where you come from
Hold her without carrying her
Accept her blessings, not her curses.

You are not your mother's body
Nor her violence, desperation, anger
You are not your father's intelligence

Nor his pride, shame, weakness.

You are your own
Pure, beautiful, fluid, strong Self.
You are the holding of all
Pure, beautiful, fluid, strong women in your lineage.

You are not the end nor the beginning
You are the middle of a flowing river
You are part of the whole.

I Wonder

What is loving?
I recall the way hummingbird kissed my forehead
I was squatting to pee
Undefended
Unprepared

She kissed me
Gently
Lightly
Then flew away
Brief kiss
Everlasting flame.

What is living?
I recall the way butterfly threaded on my body
I was laying
Naked
Hopeful

She held me
Sweetly
Assuredly
Then flew away
Short walk
Lasting power.

What is truth?
I recall the way thunder struck my power place
I was hiding
Afraid
Alone

She pierced me
Loudly

Proudly
Then went away
Lightning bolt
Flowing energy.

Now I wonder
Who am I?
Why do I live?
Why do I love?

Part III. Incorporation

You are Reborn.
You have Truth.

It is time to show up.
Back to your tribe.
Connect.
Love.

Weave the Golden Thread.
To
Yourself.
Others.
Earth.
Universe.
Yourself
Again.

Sun and The Snake

I want to feel your rays close to me
To bask in your warmth
Step closer to where I need to stand.

Without your light
I get lost in my own darkness
The pull to descend is stronger than
My will to rise
The wish to ascend is heftier than
My need to stay.

Sun,
Father of all light
Illuminate everything I feel but can't yet see
Help me dance with my shadows.

Here,
I stand naked
Like a snake just shed its skin
With wind blowing through my core
With knees shaking at the new lightness
With eyes, directly glittering at you.

Like this,
I feel your rays closer than I could before
Like this,
I feel my layers deeper than I've known before
Like this,
I thank you for changing me so lovingly

In the old skin
I would have surely died.

Forgive Me for The Things I Said

"I hope you die," I said
Slammed the door of your sporty Lexus
When you didn't answer the hundredth call I'd made in twenty
minutes
I prayed for you to live.

Who were you?
The One
Who
Twisted ugliness off my bones
Wrung clogs from my blood
Hammered desperation out my chest
Shook me till I found my own center.

Now
Under a dark sky
Lit by invisible moon
I sit by a sacred fire
Ask for forgiveness.

I
      Cast magic fishing pole
      Collect harsh words
I
      Shouted
      Texted
      Whispered
      Thought

One by one
I fish them out
From the sea of lost things.

For every catch
I send you a blessing

May you drive safely through life
May you hear no curse
May you receive gifts
May you keep the love you find.

Why I Iron

I loved ironing. It was my meditation. My church. My tradition. You at a computer on the green sofa. Me with a wireless headphone. Watching CBS Sunday Morning. Dancing around the ironing board. Playing with the iron. Stroking your shirts. As if they were your body and the iron was my hand. Smoothing wrinkles. Bringing order. Pouring my love through the spitting and snorting nose of the iron. I imagined that when you wore the shirts, you would feel my love, and draw in the energy to help you through the office days, of writing depositions, arguments, and holding your own at court.

I wanted you to feel loved, worthy, dazzling, beautiful, and powerful. I hope you did.

I still love ironing. The colorful cotton Kurtas from India. The flyaway pants hand-made by Indonesian artists. The one I wear to 5Rhythms dancing. A red Peruvian T-shirt that caught my eyes at an airport from the Amazons to Cusco. With a hummingbird.

There was a long time in between that I did not iron. I chose to wear wrinkled clothes rather than touching the iron that once represented a channel of my love. I believed that the ironed shirts somehow brought you closer to the one you met at the office, the one who was not me. I worried that it made you more attractive, approachable, smooth to her seductions. I wondered if I brought this to myself. By giving so much of myself to you, I ironed a path to my own abandonment, like a giant asphalt paver.

I swore that I will never iron another shirt for a man. I declared to all my friends so. Then I stopped ironing for myself.

Years later, I am back to ironing. Not every Sunday, but some Sundays. Not every garment but some garments. While ironing, I ask for a blessing. From the fountain of love that exists, beyond the stingy steel of the iron.

May I be generous enough to offer my love without wanting anything in return. May I give myself what I needed from others and gave to others. May I dance with my own sexiness. May I smooth my own wrinkles. May I feel my own dazzlingly beautiful authentic colors wherever I am. While crunching numbers at the office. While walking in the woods singing with the birds. While sitting quietly bathing in my tears. May I iron shirts for a worthy man one day. With all the love I have, even if I am afraid to lose him.

There is no such thing as "too much loving." There is no "irresistibly perfect ironed shirt." There is no "self-paved road to aloneness." There is an abundant love wanting to flow. There is a channel that opens, closes, opens again.

I Am Sorry I Doubted Your Love

Oh mother,
In your womb I was given life
Breath of a fire, a new beginning

Oh father,
In your strength I found possibilities
In your holding I grew to be me

I am sorry I doubted your love
I am sorry I doubted you

Oh earth,
I feel your being in my being
I love your every expression

Oh spirits,
I let your power pour over me
I surrender to your blessing

I am sorry I doubted your love
I am sorry I doubted you.

Real Cure

Our family had a mission. To stop you, my father, from drinking. Mom heard that a small dose of mouse poison can deter away attachment to alcohol. Aunt Saruul heard that an elixir from soaking the dead mouse itself in alcohol should do the trick. I had my own idea. To mix my morning urine in your beer. I was certain my urine could cure you. I was trying out a so-called "morning urine diet," a popular new-age medicine. The diet was simple. To drink all of my morning urine every day for a month. Even if it was dark orange and smelly as hell. Even if white clouds of vaginal fluids were floating in it. Even with traces of menstrual blood. Drink it all. The magazines said this diet could cure all diseases: emotional, mental, physical. I hoped the diet would make me prettier. Perhaps socially acceptable. More importantly, I hoped if the trial on me succeeded, I could cure you from your drinking disease.

A classmate with frequent migraines swore that the only cure was to rub his forehead with his mother's urine. Even Oulen Eh, Chinggis Khaan's mother, treated his battle wounds with her urine. Once, Chinggis was wounded in a faraway land and she could not send her urine. She mixed dough with her urine and sent the baked bread instead. Legend says that the bread indeed cured his wounds and he returned home. I knew of urine's healing powers. Elders often said, "Pee on it." When I had poison ivy rashes. When I cut myself with a broken glass. It was an available, accessible and free medicine. But I could not imagine rubbing mother's urine on my forehead even if a headache was pounding with weight of an iron-cast kettle. I could not let any liquid from mother touch my body, not her saliva, not her milk, nor her tears. No way. Instead, I chose to drink my own. The diet worked. First few days the urine was so dark and bitter, I could barely hold back my puke. But after few days, it got lighter and lighter. By the end of the month, it was almost as clear as water. I started drinking all my urines. It felt good.

This practice came handy years later. When I ran out of water at a vision quest, I drank my urine to keep hydrated. When a boyfriend in my early twenties wanted excitement in our intimacy, I took his pee in my mouth. He was impressed with my open sexuality, but it wasn't enough to keep his love. If one day, someone wants to piss on my face, to humiliate me, I will receive it as a medicine.

Years later, I told the story of my teenage diet to an American friend. She was so disturbed that she pulled over to look at me. We were driving to a Kirtan event to connect with the divine. "Urana, you can't tell this to anyone else," she said. "In America, no one drinks urine; it is a waste, not a nutrition. It is toxic." We are no longer friends. I hope it was not because I used to drink my pee. I disagreed with her argument without knowing why. I learned later that people with certain autoimmune diseases lose their ability to correctly extract nutrients from food and supply those nutrients to the blood stream. The body does the reverse, and all nutrients leaves their body through urine. I was diagnosed with an autoimmune condition, years after the conversation on the road. Perhaps my body had a deeper knowledge than my brain.

Father, I didn't get to try the urine medicine on you. Despite my countless imaginations and attempts in my head, I didn't have the courage to switch your beer with my golden treasure. The mouse poison was not bought, and no mouse was harmed for the curing attempt. Mom, Aunt and I tried different elixir. Tears. Words of blame. Screams of despair. Threats to leave. A silent withdrawal. Finally, a lethal giving up.

You continued to drink. On the streets seeking company of other lost souls. Alone in the kitchen. I sat shivering in my room, afraid to make any noise, wishing that the liquid in the bottle somehow turn to urine. At 19, I moved away to another country, to start a new life. Liberated, renewed. I never considered going back. One fall, when I brought my then-boyfriend later-husband to Mongolia, you came to greet us in the hotel. You opened a briefcase to reveal a big bottle of Chinggis beer—the Mongolian equivalent of Guinness. "It is for breakfast," you said. Yes, beer is milk, wine is dessert, vodka and whiskey are the real meal. In your world. I felt ashamed. Afraid that my boyfriend would love me less because of my hopeless father. I swore to never come back to Mongolia.

Now, I've lived through a broken leg, a broken marriage, a lost child, multiple unsuccessful fertility treatments, difficult bosses and heart-breaking relationships. I've sought healing from yoga, meditation, plants, lands, oils, crystals, mantras, drums, rattles, singing bowls, voices, dances, reiki and shamans. I know now that the only true medicine is Love. I know now that it wasn't Oulun Eh's urine that healed Chinggis Khaan; it was her love. It was my own self-love, ability to receive all my dirties that transformed me, not the morning liquid itself. By taking in what is discarded by the world as useless waste, I managed to turn myself into purity of water.

I wish I knew it then. I wish I had poured my love to your cup instead of an imaginary golden elixir. I wish I had the courage to walk into the kitchen, put my hands on your shoulder and tell you all the things I felt and you deserved to hear. "I know you are hurting and ashamed and it is okay. I am here with you and I love you."

I am sorry. I was too small.

I barely made it to your funeral. You died on a Friday evening in a cold January, thousands of miles away. Mom called me Saturday morning around 10 a.m. I was leaving an acupuncture treatment in Georgetown. "Don't worry about coming to the funeral. It is on Monday morning and you won't make it anyway," she said. I called every airline and travel agency I could find, bought myself a ticket, packed my things, and left my apartment the same afternoon. After 28 hours, three layovers in California, Germany, Russia, and $10,000 dollars, I landed in an icy field of Chinggis Khaan airport. A relative picked me up and we drove straight to a hilltop facility where your cremation took place. I got to see your face before a sacred fire turned you to ashes. With prematurely sunken bones, wrinkled brown skin, you looked old and tired. I wondered why I was afraid of you all these years. You were almost as small as me. I poured milk over your body and burned incense for your soul. Whispered "Hello" and "Goodbye." Mother handed me a plastic folder filled with papers. "I found it under his bed. Must have been waiting to give you."

I could not open the folder then. When I opened it a few years later in the living room of my Virginia apartment, I couldn't help but cry. A copy of my high school diploma. A letter of recommendation you drafted for a teacher to sign when I was accepted to study in Japan on a scholarship. A certificate of excellence in middle school. A Xerox copy of silver and bronze medals I won as a teenager at national physics Olympiad. Letters and cards I sent from Osaka. Baby photos of me. Family portraits. A copy of an Australian newspaper, where I was featured on the front page, when I attended a jamboree of the Asia-Pacific scouts. A medical record book with Russian and Latin writings that I fail to comprehend. All of my childhood and teenage years I had left behind were in that folder. You kept them safe. To remind me one day where I come from. You preserved them with care. Even when I had abandoned my past and you along with it. It was you who held your love for me all these years. Through the unanswered calls, unbequethed visits, unsent prayers. Your love survived the bottles that helped you ease your pain, the shame that separated us more than the continents, my pride that blinded me to believe I was better off without you.

I thank you for your love. I thank you for your ever-persevering trust. That one day I would come back.

Now when you visit me in my dreams, I open my purse and take out a bottle of offering. It is not filled with beer or pee. It is filled with my love for you. The love I could not pour for you when you were alive. I trust that you receive this offering, in the place where your spirit now resides. You smile at me and ask, "Is this for breakfast?"

A New Day

When in a desert
A strong wind caresses you without consent
Learn how to
Bend backwards
Grow sideways
Like the ancient trees
Harvest wind's power
Like the giant windmills.

Grow large feet
Like the camels
Walk in sand without sinking
Wear a waxy coat
Like the cacti
Preserve the water of life inside.

Every moment
A new beginning
Every sneeze
A little death.

Bless you.

Every morning
Yesterday cedes
Today emerges anew
Surprise, delight, wonder, bewilderment
Tears, joy, more sneezes.
Nothing is the same
From one moment to the other.

Every breath
A part of me dies
Another is born.

This day
Just like many others
A day.

This day
Unlike any other
A new day.

Leaves to Seeds

Fallen leaves
Can dance
All they need is to
Lean into the wind.

Let the breeze carry you
You've been a part of a tree
Now you are with the wind
To the earth you will return
Become humus for
New seed to grow.

Rejoicing of My Rebirth

The third time I was born
Joy blazed
Sun blessed
The grassy field

Butterflies, big and small
Fluttered around my head
Flowers, colors so bright
Birds chirping.

Animals gathered
Showered me with loving gaze
Trees held space
Sheltered me with grace.

I am beautiful
I am wanted
I am loved
I am free.

A gift to the world.

No matter that
I could not feel my mother nor my own body.

I am the child of Nature
Red lava of her core burns within me
Jagged edges of her bone make my spine
Flurry blows of her breathe untangle my hair
Tears of her compassion wash away my pain

Fierce arrow of her eyes thunders me awake
Firm holding of her branches anchors me alive

Mycelium of her fiber threads through me
Humus of her flesh feeds my being.

I belong in this wild openness
With my bodiless, motherless beauty.

Sweet Lover

Morning sun on my breasts
My nipples on fire
No lover's hand can evoke me like this

My chest leaps towards its warm caress
Free from my wiry ribs
Rays of my own hands glide across the velvety mount
Dancing with sunrays.

Voices in my head:
"Men don't like it." "Too rich taste."
"Shower, soap, mask your aroma in mass-produced perfume."
"Eat a pineapple to make you sweeter."
"Don't please men, until they go down on you first."

This noise
Crowds out the sounds that matter
Chirping birds, humming bees
Buzzing grasshoppers.

Must I
Pour honey near entrance, to allure a bear to cave?
Top with whipped cream, to seduce a hungry child?

Must I
Measure his generosity
By skills of his tongue?

Nothing but water for four days
No men, women, pet to keep me from myself
My own hands
Tread tenderness of this estranged temple.

Ring the bell gently
You are invited
You belong
You bring bounty.

Make small steps
Bow like a Zen master
Layer by layer
Slide door
Unveil curtain
Beaded, bambooed, silky, velvety

Explore with
Curiosity of Marco
Courage of Chinggis
Humility of a student new to the arts.

Wake the dormant volcano to pulse and shake
Fill you with fiery fresh waters.

Let it flow
Let it flow
Like a river
Down your firm limbs to your toes buried in grass.

I am sweet
Bees tell me so
Ants lick me so
Hummingbirds kiss me so.

I am a sweet lover to all.

No pine
No honey
No whip
No soap

Just my essence.

White Puffy Jacket

I am looking at a photo from my first year in college. Against a backdrop of snow, boys and girls smile at the photographer. I recall names of some of them. Some are nameless figures with whom I shared a classroom and teachers once. But I recognize their expensive puffy jackets. Purple, black, red and blue. Thick and warm. Properly manufactured. Probably some good brands. I find myself, in a white puffy jacket, thinner than the other jackets. At first, it brings a flash of shame to my face. Then a sorrow. Followed by a deep gratitude.

My mother made this jacket. She couldn't afford to buy me a new one. The outer shell is a used white raincoat, donated by American missionaries. Maybe it was the Red Cross. Can't recall. It had English words sewn in red threads, that landed above my left breast. The lining is a retired grey satin, previously hugged by mom's good coat for over 20 years. The filling is foam resurrected from father's winter pants. Mom sewed the jacket over several days, hunching over the sewing machine, stepping on the petals with energy of a charging bull. She made a dusty blue one for my older brother, and a black one for her youngest. Short puffy jackets were in fashion in the modern Ulaanbaatar, a town recovering from collapse of Communism five years ago. New rich were rising, traders between China and Russia, gold and copper discoverers of the booming mining industry, new landowners.

My country of nomads, where the land belonged to no one and served everyone, was changing rapidly. My family was still poor. Mom was running a small cafeteria. Aunt Selenge was the cook. I was the waiter. Dad was looking for a job, but his search always ended up in an empty bottle. We still lived from loan to loan, from a pawn shop nearby, where my mother's gold earrings took a permanent housing. The loan and cafeteria cash covered our textbooks and fed our bellies. But there was no extra left for fancy new clothes. I had good grades and can-do attitude and got a government scholarship. It allowed me to go to college. The classes were full of kids from the new rich families.

When fall arrived, my heart sank. Everyone in school was wearing fashionable down jackets. I had just turned 18 and I wanted to be noticed by boys. In high school, I didn't mind all that much that I only wore hand-me-downs from someone in the family. Now, I was a woman and wanted to look like one. Mom understood that. She had been 18 once too, wishing for a long wool coat in checkered patterns. That week, she created three cloaks of invisibility for her children. Mine was white. With red threads over the left breast line. It made me unnoticeable by those who can't see beyond the surface. It taught me that trying to fit in a tribe wearing a mask eats away at my true belonging.

Mother, your actions expressed what your words couldn't. It was easy to see the bitch in you. But I couldn't recognize the mother wolf. It was easy to notice your coarseness when you dragged 80 pounds of garlic across the China-Mongolia border. But I didn't respect the strength it took. It was easy to point out imperfections of the white jacket. But I didn't appreciate its true value.

Since then I have bought many short puffy jackets. Purple, black, red and blue. Thick and warm. Properly manufactured. Some good brands. The thin red one I bought the first year in Japan. The bright orange one that warmed me on mountain tops of Machu Picchu and Mount Shasta. The black hooded one with furry rims that I wore to my first date with the sexy Hungarian. But I wish I had kept the white one you made.

To the Darkness Where I Belong

Sky darkens, clouds emerge
Thunder strikes
Once, twice, three times
You look at me
Light shines
Once, twice, countless times.

Oh, sacred medicine
Breath of life, from your heart to mine, through the
blessed pipe.

To this primordial darkness I must go
To be held
To begin again.

Fog lifts, harmonica opens the way
Tears flow
No fear, trust in love.

I bow at your feet
Weight of your arms
Just the right heaviness
Just the right lightness
Just right.

We don't know
Why path unfolds the way it does
Why hearts open, close, then open again
We don't know
Where sacred song calls us toward.

Lean in
Let the medicine embody you

Let the sound open the way
Clouds emerge
Thunder strikes, again
Power turns off then on again.

Darkness
Where I belong
I am no longer afraid of you.
I know you will hold me
With a sweet sound of harmonica and a kiss from a Beloved.

Arrival of Light, Sound, and Other Reckonings

There is a reckoning
A smile, a sound, an accidental touch
While playing a hand that guarantees losing

You remember at once
Don't know exactly
What
When
Where
The memory is felt.

The next moment
Your hand reaches for the hand of the One
As if it is the most natural thing
As if your whole life was in search of this moment
As if waiting is simply impossible

Even if
The hand you hold is promised to the Other
The heart you hear is bound to yet Another
Even if
Everyone else
Doubts the magic you know
Drops it in the laundry basket from yesterday's love
Even if
The odds are against you.

Dancing with you was like remembering the time
I was a goddess
You a god
Flowing in perfect unison

Each fiber of us in sync
With each other
With the source.

Kissing you was like drinking from
The magic cup
Waterfall
Wherever else sweet juice of life is stored
A place
I never believed I could find
I never thought I would be allowed in.

Hugging you was like finding my place in the world
Warm, cozy
Tingly, sparkling
That perfect place
Where I
Awake while asleep
Rest while create
Where I
Belong.

Parting from you was like a twist in a thriller
Body whirls
Anticipation, confusion, guessing
Knowing, excited, despaired
Inside shouting
Outside speechless.

"Why such chemistry, so fast?" you say
Because our bodies know the jewels within us
In resonance with each other's currents.

"Why such bad timing?" you say
Because the timing is always divine
Trust, surrender, hope is the only way to align.

You were right
The sound and the light
Arrived at the same time

Now I sit
In a dark silence
Remembering.

On one, two, three
We both let go.

The Sound of You

The sound of you woke something in me
A tune from another life where
You promised to find
Me
Again.

Hidden echoes in the rocks of a sacred mountain
Inaccessible
Insurmountable
Unimaginable

Secrets carved in the walls
Deep
Dark
Cave.

I've been asleep
So long
Could not remember the songs
Of my own sweet heart
I haven't eaten an apple
Nor have I drunk a potion

Was it a spell?

But your sound
So familiar
Learnt and forgotten
So deep yet so near

Struck chord
Torn veil
Covering entrance of
Deep

Dark
Cave.

Where black bear sleeps
Waiting for spring that never comes
Dreaming of sweet honey
Flowing from the chamber.

Measurements

Five hours we've spent together
    Including the time in cars, bathrooms, in-between places
    Four hours I heard the music of your voice
    Less all the breathing, eating, wiping of mouths and noses.

Three hours or so, I looked into your eyes
    Accounting for moments of blinking, blushing, looking up
        and down
    Ten more minutes, I could have seen your beautiful face
    If I only drove a little faster, just by a ten mile an hour or so
    Had I learnt how to drive with one hand seven years
        ago
    I could have held yours with my free hand.

Four thousand miles, is how far you live as per the crow flies
    I could not get there by foot even if I had the strength to
        walk the distance
    Six hours ahead, is when you greet the rising sun
    Cutting down the time we could be awake together by one
        quarter.

    Several years late, is when you appeared in my life
    I could have been prettier, younger, more innocent

Short was our embrace, even if the intensity felt like a lifetime
    Stupid was I, to not hold your hand a little longer, or be bold
        enough to kiss you
    Three months at least, is time we must wait to see if this is real
    Few times before the loving presence took over our senses
        and we mistook it for romance.

Ninety minutes of a flight could bring us together, if you lived
   in Sri Lanka and I in India
   Slightly longer than my daily commute to the office
      Five more hours, I could see you, if I ever fly through
      Frankfurt again.

On and on and on, my mind goes
   Counting, calculating, analyzing, devising, planning,
   daydreaming

I forget the state of my heart simply full of joy
   I move away from the absolute truth that
   Even if this was the only time we meet, it is enough.

   I was born already loving you
   I will be born again loving you.

Hummingbird Called

Hummingbird called
Asked for help
I got in my car
Drove to darkness

Blinding rain pounds the windows
Burning engine scorches my feet
Thunder threatens
Commands to stop
Angels' voice inside
Calls to carry on.

I walk into a room
Where wounded bird lies
I see you sitting
There in left corner

Lullaby carries white compassion
Bells and bowls ring crystal tones
Ancestors rattle, drum, whistle
Together we cry and caress.

Sound of creation
Flows through me
Words of wisdom
Flow through you

We survive the night
Hummingbird lives
You leave
Old me depart.

Was it your arrival

Thunder announced
Rain blessed
Angels cheered?
Was it you
Hummingbird called me toward?

To Find You Again

The dress unbuttons itself
The hooks part, straps leave
Willingly.
Every inch of me desires
To be naked
Melt into the beauty of your
Threshold.

Your parted lips emit sweetest call
Invite me to the sacred land inside.

I become a little bird
Fly into the cave of your mouth
Wings brush against the walls of your teeth
Feel the carvings from eons ago
Imprints of your soul
Waited till this day
To be discovered
To be remembered.

I become a little fish
Swim in the ocean of your saliva
Circle the peninsula of your tongue
Dive beneath
Feel soft membranes of your tissue
Pulsating with lava of life.

Wake up
Wake up!
I've found you
Again.

I can't hold back this longing

Ancient desire, primal instinct
Stronger than walls I built to hide in
Frame breaks
Beauty emerges
From the fires within my core.

I want to become small enough
To nest in your belly
Leave a tiny mark
To find you
Again.

Gratitude

You gaze at me
Sitting on edge of the bed
Still warm from morning lovemaking.

The light in your eyes
Tug a string in my heart
Lift a rock covering a tiny spring.

Sweet waters bubble
Flow down my cheeks
Turn into a whisper in my mouth.
A silent
"Thank you."

The sock you lost
Hides underneath the sham
It wanted to stay with me
Bearing your scent.

Game I Want to Play

Playing with you is not like a ping pong, badminton, tennis or squash
Where ball is passed between humans, from human to wall, from wall to human
Bouncing in reaction, fast, with much force, exertion.

The winner is the one who runs fastest, applies forces the right way
The one who can stress you, hit your weakest spots
Cunningly, in an angle unexpected.

Playing with you is like letting a balloon in the air
To float free carried by the breeze
You catch, examine, sit with, then return it to me

Only the balloon emerges transformed,
Into a brighter color
With magic patterns added
Having touched your hands and wisdom
Nurtured in the mastery of your quiet reflection.

Engaging with you is not like a tug-o-war or wrestle in the mud
No sweating, bleeding, screaming
No tumbling, kicking, scraping of knees, twisting of ankles.

Engaging with you is like swimming the deep ocean with the dolphins
Moving gently, never rushed but always with a purpose
Whole school in togetherness
Smooth glides
Deep dives
Thoroughly seen
Truly listened to.

Being with you is nothing like a puppet show
No strings pulling and tugging against one's wills
No one talking without moving lips
No mouths moved by invisible hands
So that others can get confused and laugh.

Being with you is like flying a kite in the sky on a sandy beach
Feet on the ground, next to each other
Spirits high above, riding the wind
Flowing and dancing
Crossing clouds
Clearing fogs
Reaching for the sun's warm rays.

This is a game I had not played before

No instant gratifications, loud spectators
No applauding, cheering, booing
No competition, winners, losers
No trophies, medals, uniforms.

Through a Zen master's holding, observing, absorbing
A koan is whispered to bamboo forest
The answer finds you in vibrant dreams

Through monk's silent tending
A seed of creation blooms into a fragrant flower
Wakes the hermit from
A lonely contemplation in a darkened cave.

This is a game I want to play for eternity.

Rivers of Your Palm

Three rivers on your palm
Take me to a sacred place
I visit in my dreams
Where three streams merge to one.

Or do they emerge from one?

One with gently flowing waters
Singing a lullaby
Calming presence
Like a violin

Another with galloping foamy waters
Fresh springs
Waking the world
Creating newness
Like a flute

The other with ever changing presence
Sometimes flooding
Sometimes roaring
Dark waters, rocky flows
Like a drum.

Such divergences contained in one palm
How do they come from the same place?
Meet into oneness?
What divine blessings
Do your waters carry?
In which river
Shall I bathe today?

You say that one of the rivers is

An after-mark of a surgical cut
To save a finger that wanted to
Float away into nothingness.

But now it flows so beautifully
With the other two
Together they transmit healing light
To those who you touch.

This teaches me
Not to shun my darkest sides
Nor resent the painful events
But to
Accept
Reconstruct
Mend
Heal.

Then my flaws
Rebirth as a river
Meet my gifts
At a sacred shore
Create
A perfect symphony.

Blessings

Out of shower, hair wet
Body wrapped in a towel
I find you on a couch
With tears in your eyes

Your sister's cat left this world
The last time you held her
You knew
It would be the last.
What else do you know?

You say a blessing
Light a single candle
I hold your head
In my chest
Say a blessing
For her
For your sister
For you.

May we light a candle for
Everyone we've ever loved and lost
To adorn the darkness
Like the stars in the night sky

May we shed a tear for
Everyone we've ever held and let go
To quench thirst of every heart
Now and then.

Eat bread, cheese, berries
Drink the tea that waited all night
A table separates us
Like a continent between

A moment of silence.

Your arms call me
To your lap
Happy to land there

I could rest
Here
Like this
Forever
Kissing your face
Every inch precious.

You point to your third eye
My lips bless your light
A thousand blessings return

May you be loved
Always
May I be loved
Always
May we hold each other
Again.

Candles in My Heart

We enter gates of a temple
Many before us have come to pray
To seek shelter, forgiveness, redemption
To find love, a will to live.

Grief weighs in my heart like anchor of abandoned ship
Lost, nowhere to sail, nowhere to stay
People watch from ashore, wonder whether to enter
Brave peeks, no one stays
Happy ones avoid, know imminent death awaits
Death of old satisfying beliefs

Ones aboard walk tensely, not to break eggshells
Not to wake sleeping giants in hidden corners.

This is how I saw myself
This is how many saw me
This is how you saw me too
But this is not how I am.

I kneel in front of the great mother
Crying over her dying son's stigma-bloody body
I too weep, weep, weep
My tears merge with hers
She holds me
In her arms
With her son
Just like her son.

I belong to love
I belong to tenderness
I belong to forgiveness
I belong to light

I belong.

I light a single candle for her compassion
Stroke sands of new beginnings
With shaky fingers
Baby candle, abandoned
Emerges
Gift of a life, awaiting my touch

I lit her with fires of my own flesh
Whisper prayer to this belonging
To her
With her
With myself
Family is created from a wax and wick
Lights up darkest corners of my heart.

You visit altar of my new home
Say prayer in your quiet way
I see you
Through curtains of my tears
Pouring monsoon in a hot Indian summer
I pray
For each candle you lit in my heart.

I now know why they built Taj Mahal.

How Love Finds You

Sometimes
Love hits you like a comet
You don't see it coming
Feel its impact after it has fallen
Changed your being
Turned it upside down, inside out.

Rivers dried, lives gone, sky darkened
Fire ignited, forests fried
Lands cleared with storms of passion
New richness found
In darkest soil, deepest water.

So much to grow
Possibilities
After
So much death and sad goodbyes.

Sometimes
Love creeps in silently
Through cracks in your heart
While you are half asleep
Dreaming of
A future
With someone else
Who flies in like a star
Shining light of angels.

It fills your space, your being
With small drops
You don't notice until
Deep in
Sometimes floating
Occasionally sinking

Always held
Under pressure
Above pleasure.

Rarely,
Love finds you
Exactly where you are
As if a fog has lifted
Blinders removed
As if you
Suddenly woke up
From deep sleep.

You find Yourself
Exactly
Where you are meant to be.

Wanting
Nothing less
Nothing more
As if for the first time
You see the all of You
With its
Dry lands
Flooding rivers
Burning forests
Darkened skies
Glittering moons.

Open to the
Now
and the
New
Holding the
Then, there, therefore.

All your lovers
Surrounding you
Watching you
Wanting you.

Once for all
Fully surrendered
Thoroughly loved
Utterly
Uniquely
You.

Goose Calls

Hello,
    Goose said.
    Sitting on rims of my balcony
    Singing unknown tune.

What a place to land
    In this urban jungle
    Tenth floor of a concrete castle
    What a way to wake up
    On this cold Saturday
    Tenth day of turning leaves.

Have you come
    To call me to my ancestors?
    Have you just marked
    Certainty of my waking?

Orange Horses Are My Best Friends

There is a painting on my office wall. Of orange horses running through a green field. Blue mountains with snowy tops. The greens, blues and oranges are so bright, almost neon. It was a wedding gift from my younger brother and his classmates. "It is too ugly to hang in the apartment," he said. "Maybe in a basement, when we get a house." At the time I sat in a cubicle at work, so the painting was left rolled inside a plastic container. It was too beautiful to be thrown away.

The house was never bought. The man with superior taste in art is gone. The same apartment where I now live alone has too many other things on the walls. But now I have an office, and the painting lives there proudly.

"The proportions in this painting are unrealistic," said a colleague. He is an amateur painter. Yes, the horses are too large compared to the nomadic Ger behind. Their feet are off the ground. "Colors are way off," he continued. Yes, there aren't many bright orange horses and neon green fields. Not in this reality. But I always loved the painting. It brought smiles to my face when I returned from a tense meeting. It gave me hope when I struggled with a project that was going nowhere. It helped me dream when I was upset at a co-worker's accusatory comments on an email I sent.

I believe that every gift we receive carries a medicine. Perhaps not visible at first, but later, when our eyes and hearts are open. I understood the medicine of this painting years after it was given to me. Ancestors visited my dreams asking me to wake up. They would gallop on horses, beat drums to my heart, fly a flag and point to some distant point. I resisted with all my might. "I am an educated professional," I said. "I have a job, responsibilities, an urban life. A dream of a better future where

I live in a decent size house with a real family." But the ancestors are quite stubborn. They insisted that my main responsibility is to carry forward the medicine of the lineage. When I didn't listen, my body suffered. Constant fatigue, frequent cold sores, runny noses. Finally, mysterious red rashes all over my body. After numerous visits to specialists, I was diagnosed with an autoimmune disease. Physically, autoimmune disease indicates that my immune system attacks its own healthy cells mistaking them for harmful aliens. Energetically, it reflects an inner conflict, a war, with my own body. I am not qualified to explain what the medical cause is. But my intuition tells me that it is caused by an incongruence within me. I searched deep inside. I realized that I was living a dual life.

Externally, I was an accomplished economist and an accountant, who measured most things by numbers, currencies, and economic values. Internally, I was a shaman who traveled between dimensions, where a concept of time and place does not exist. The only currency in the other reality is abundant love or the lack of it. I surrendered to my ancestral calling. I was initiated to shaman's path, paved by my lineage long before I was born. At first, I received healing from other shamans. Then I started learning from some. I eventually connected with my own helping spirits. In shamanism, helping spirits are animal allies that accompany a shaman to non-ordinary reality and provide protection and teachings. My helping spirits appeared in various shapes and colors. On a computer screen. In a TV show. During walk in the woods. While I slept. On postcards. On strangers' shirts, dresses, purses. They gave me feathers, bones, furs, and droppings. My little apartment filled with their gifts; left no room for the orange horses. Their gifts were numerous. One brought me songs. The other a courage to speak the truth. Another a protection. Yet another a vision.

Then came the horses. I started shamanic journeying for others. They help me travel to other dimensions to retrieve departed or stolen souls. They are bright orange too.

What guided me in life was not visible to me. Maybe it was visible to my younger brother. Maybe he just liked bright orange horses. One thing I now know is that the guidance is always here with us. We see them only through the eyes of an open heart.

Now, the orange horses run the green fields of my office. Alongside a purple bridge over blue water lilies, a small house in a shiny pink sky, a giant tree among the clouds with red and white flowers, colorful swirls and bursting stars, and a large flower with multi-colored petals that looks more like a headpiece for a native chief than a flower. These were "painted" by me. At one of those "sip and paint" events. When I was much younger, I copied masterpieces by Van Gogh and Monet. Sometimes followed my own inner images. I didn't know then that I was painting my own medicine and spirit allies.

Now, I am at peace with my dual existence. The analyzing, calculating, decision-making CPA is an honorable part of me. So is the dreaming shaman who sees magic in everything. I smile "Hello" to the horses, houses, flowers, bridges, trees every Monday through Friday. As I smile "Hello" to the computer, chair, the papers, notebooks. They all belong.

"It is the most realistic and beautiful painting," I say to my colleague. "But only for those who see beyond the ordinary."

Universe Is Inside

When my jaw tightens
Doors to heavens close
When my brows furrow closer
Kingdom of magic moves farther.

When I sneeze
Irritated with the sourness of the world
A single golden leaf falls into abyss
From a tree of wisdom.

Center of this universe is
In my own heart
Divided by dark caves
Flooded by roaring rivers.

The moon there is beautiful
In all its phases
Even in its
Total eclipse.

I Am the Poem

I had a dream. That my true love will write me a poem. It became a yard stick I used to measure the strength of a man's love. It became a proof of my own value. To be worthy of a poem. To be a muse, not amusement.

My heart broke when I discovered the poems you wrote for her. In the journal kept at your bedside. The one I never imagined opening. The one I never would have opened. That morning, two days before you moved out, I opened the journal while you were showering. Something inside me said I must. To know the truth. The one I refused to see. To unveil a shadow that I lived with.

The poems were beautiful. Full of longing. About perfectly lucent skins and plump kissable lips. About shimmering eyes and flaming hearts. About deep desires and destined lovers. I took photos of the pages and put the journal back in your bag. Made of dark leather. The one I gifted you at our last anniversary. To make you look dashing. To go with the sexy suits, I selected for you. I didn't know the truth of your heart then.

I cried for days when you left. I cried for months. I cried for years. I didn't know if I was crying because you betrayed me, or because you abandoned me, or because you never wrote a poem for me.

The first man who wrote me a poem took me by surprise. He was a wild and alive soul; merely 20 years old. My buddy at a vision quest. In the mountains of Colorado, in a circle attending the School of Lost Borders. Over four days of "no food," "no walls," and "no human contacts," he was my buddy. A lifeline. My only connection to the world outside. He did the morning check-ins. I did the evenings. One stone was left each time, at our "buddy pile." His stones with green moss, mine with orange. To signal that we are alive and well. To each other. With each other.

The poem he wrote me was not a typical love poem. Not about kissing my lips or caressing my body. But about seeing me for who I am. Not about dreaming and wanting to be my lover. But about hearing my true longings and witnessing my rebirth. As a friend, as a brother, as a tribe.

Once he left me a letter at the buddy pile. Then a rusted soda-can filled with fresh wildflowers. The can resides over a fireplace in my apartment. Wildflowers are still inside, no longer fresh and naïve but dried and wised. They remind me that I am loved. That someone cares enough to write a poem. Someone cares enough to pluck tiny flowers from a green field and to deliver them in a can of perseverance.

I returned to the same mountains two years later. After falling in love with someone who promised me the world. To build a house of my dreams. To have children. To stay together through thick and thin. This beautiful man - a perfect couch potato - vowed to hike the Inca trail to Machu Picchu with me. It did not happen. I hiked the Incas alone. I danced with the condor alone. I greeted the deer at heart-shaped lake alone. All my dreams, in their blind hopefulness and fragile illusions, were shattered.

I returned to the mountains to find a true source of love. Not the one I placed in a man's love. Not the one I expected to arrive in a poem. I still lived in the apartment with a fireplace guarded by a rusted can full of wildflowers. I didn't have children, except the tantrum throwing and spiteful ones in my heart.

I received from the mountains everything I asked for. More than I hoped for. I fell in love with every single person in the circle, old and young, man and woman, teacher and student, alike. I wrote my first book–hand-bound love letters written to the people in the circle. Poems there came from a deeper source of love.

I realized that someone had been writing poems for me all along.

Not in words about kissable lips and milky skins. Instead, in the songs of blue birds. In the calligraphy of white clouds. In the dance of green grasses. In the golden webs of tireless spiders.

Wanderer, Listen

You've been searching for a true love
But all loves are true.

Inside you
All the water you are thirsty for
Inside you
All the warmth you seek from the sun.

Mind and Heart

My dear restless mind
Do not swim against the currents of my heart.
Bless you. Stop.

I am loved beyond your knowing.

Acknowledgments

Some poems in this book were first published in:

"Why I Iron" in *Chaleur Magazine*

"The House You Didn't Build for Us" in *Cathexis Northwest Press*

"Games We Played" and "Game I Want to Play" in *Meat for Tea*

"How far can you run?", "A kiss remembered", and "Cats, Husbands, Fathers" in *Riza Press Multimedia Poetry and Art Journal*

"Cats, Husbands, Fathers" starts with a paragraph prompt provided by Suzi Tucker at a writing retreat. Much gratitude to Suzi for the inspiration.

I am grateful for comments from Anatoly Kazakov, Carolyn Flynn, Erik Desrosiers, Francesco Ciriaci, Lea Sloan, Marie Rodriguez, Robert Haferd, Suzi Tucker, Vladimir Inozemsev, and William Prince on early drafts of this collection. Much heart-felt appreciation to Ruth Wharton, Pedro McMillan, and Larry Hobbs, who guided my journey through Severance, Threshold, and Incorporation phases.

Above all, this collection was birthed through love and encouragement of Erik Desrosiers. Thank you for weaving the golden threads with me.

About Atmosphere Press

Atmosphere Press is an independent, full-service publisher for excellent books in all genres and for all audiences. Learn more about what we do at atmospherepress.com.

We encourage you to check out some of Atmosphere's latest releases, which are available at Amazon.com and via order from your local bookstore:

Big Man Small Europe, poetry by Tristan Niskanen
You are the Moon, a picture book by Shana Rachel Diot
In the Cloakroom of Proper Musings, a lyric narrative by Kristina Moriconi
The Glorious Between, a novel by Doug Reid
Chasing the Dragon's Tail, nonfiction by Craig Fullerton
The Unordering of Days, poetry by Jessica Palmer
It's Not About You, poetry by Daniel Casey
A Dream of Wide Water, poetry by Sharon Whitehill
The Sacrifice Zone, a novel by Roger S. Gottlieb
Radical Dances of the Ferocious Kind, poetry by Tina Tru
The Woods Hold Us, poetry by Makani Speier-Brito
My Cemetery Friends: A Garden of Encounters at Mount Saint Mary in Queens, New York, nonfiction and poetry by Vincent J. Tomeo
Report from the Sea of Moisture, poetry by Stuart Jay Silverman
White Snake Diary, nonfiction by Jane P. Perry

About the Author

Uranbileg Batjargal was born in Mongolia. It is the country of horsemen, warriors, conquerors, nomads who travel camelback, shamans who communicate with worlds and dimensions beyond the ordinary reality. As a young person, she loved climbing barefoot on the rocky hills, gathering wild berries, conversing with small birds, and singing out loud in the open summer sky.

Uranbileg left Mongolia when she was 19 to study in Japan, where she became immersed in the contemplative arts. She graduated from the University of Tokyo with a Master's degree in Economics and moved to the United States to pursue a career at the World Bank. Along the way, she was married—and divorced. Brokenhearted, she renewed her connection to the mystical realms through meditation and other contemplative energy practices. She completed three vision quests informed by the Native American tradition of celebrating the coming of age and starting of a new life. Those vision quests changed her life inalterably and continue to guide her work today.

Today, Uranbileg walks in two worlds. As an economist, a business officer, and a certified public accountant, she makes a living by managing budgets and performance reporting and applying data governance strategy and principles. In her other world, she is a poet, a meditation teacher, and a practitioner of healing arts.

Uranbileg's poetry is filled with rebellion against the ordinary, longing for freedom and love, and returning to roots. Uranbileg invites us to investigate what in our lives is ready to die; how we can make a companion of patience as we witness the old gradually giving way to the new; and ways we may embrace rebirth with the love and strength that all newborns need and deserve to receive.

CPSIA information can be obtained
at www.ICGtesting.com
Printed in the USA
LVHW052243031220
673227LV00023B/4040